The Castles of Cheshire

by
P.W. Cullen and R. Hordern

Crossbow Books

First Published 1986

Acknowledgements

The authors wish to thank Mr K. Hordern and Mrs L. Sharp.

Photographs of Pevensey Castle, Restormel Castle and Orford Castle. (Copyright Historic Buildings and Monuments Commission for England).

Photograph of Beaumaris Castle (Wales Tourist Board).

All illustrations not acknowledged are from the Crossbow Collection.

CONTENTS

LIST OF ILLUSTRATIONS

Fig. 1 Map of Cheshire in 1066.
Fig. 2 Anglo-Saxon Chester.
Fig. 3 Castle shown on the Bayeux Tapestry.
Fig. 4 Motte and bailey castle and surrounding village.
Fig. 5 Map showing the location of Cheshire's castles.
Fig. 6 Aerial photograph of Aldford castle. (Air views)
Fig. 7 Aerial photograph of Malpas castle. (Air views)
Fig. 8 Early nineteenth century print of Halton castle.
Fig. 9 The Agricola tower, Chester. (Copyright Historic Buildings and Monuments Commission for England).
Fig.10 Reconstruction of Chester castle in the early fourteenth century.
Fig.11 Print of sixteenth century plan of Chester castle.
Fig.12 Early nineteenth century print of Chester castle's thirteenth century hall.
Fig.13 Aerial photograph of Chester castle. (Air views)
Fig.14 Eastgate, Chester.
Fig.15 Reconstruction of Beeston's inner ward in 1225.
Fig.16 Beeston castle in the early fourteenth century.
Fig.17 Cross section through the gatehouse of the inner ward at Beeston.
Fig.18 View of the gatehouse from the interior of the inner ward after reconstruction.
Fig.19 Open backed tower along the line of the curtain wall.
Fig.20 Drawbridge system before reconstruction in 1303/4.
Fig.21 Hoarding at Beeston.
Fig.22 Beeston castle during the Civil War.
Fig.23 Map of Cheshire during the English Civil War.
Fig.24 The battle of Rowton Moor.

Preface.

This book begins with the emergence of the shire or county of Cheshire as an administrative unit in the tenth century. The county was developed around the Anglo-Saxon burh at Chester which took the form of a fortified town.

After the Norman Conquest a succession of powerful Earls developed the county institutions. Although the crown eventually took the county it retained a separate, privileged, administrative status as a Palatinate.

The castles of Cheshire built after the conquest played their part in the consolidation of Norman control, particularly in view of the threat from Wales. The Earl's main seat, Chester castle, was the centre of the county administration but most were private feudal strongholds acting as links in the chain of authority within Cheshire.

The English conquest of Wales, and the creation of the county of Flintshire in 1284 resulted in the stabilisation of Cheshire's western boundary along the line of the River Dee. The county boundaries remained largely unchanged from the thirteenth century until 1974. Since the pre-1974 boundaries of Cheshire relate more to the political structure within which the castles were built we have kept within their limits for this work (Fig. 1).

The improvement of internal national security and closer Royal supervision of the county had made many of the castles redundant by the sixteenth century. Some were hastily repaired during the English Civil War of the seventeenth century, a war which witnessed their destruction as military strongholds.

The most extensive surviving fortifications are found at Beeston and Chester but less well known are the gently rounded earthworks, found throughout the county, that mark the sites of motte and bailey castles.

We are grateful to all those who have assisted our efforts, in particular the staff of the City of Chester Record Office, the County Record Office and the Chester City Library. Thanks are also due to Dr Grahame Webster for reading our draft and providing some useful suggestions and encouragement.

P.W.C. and R.H.

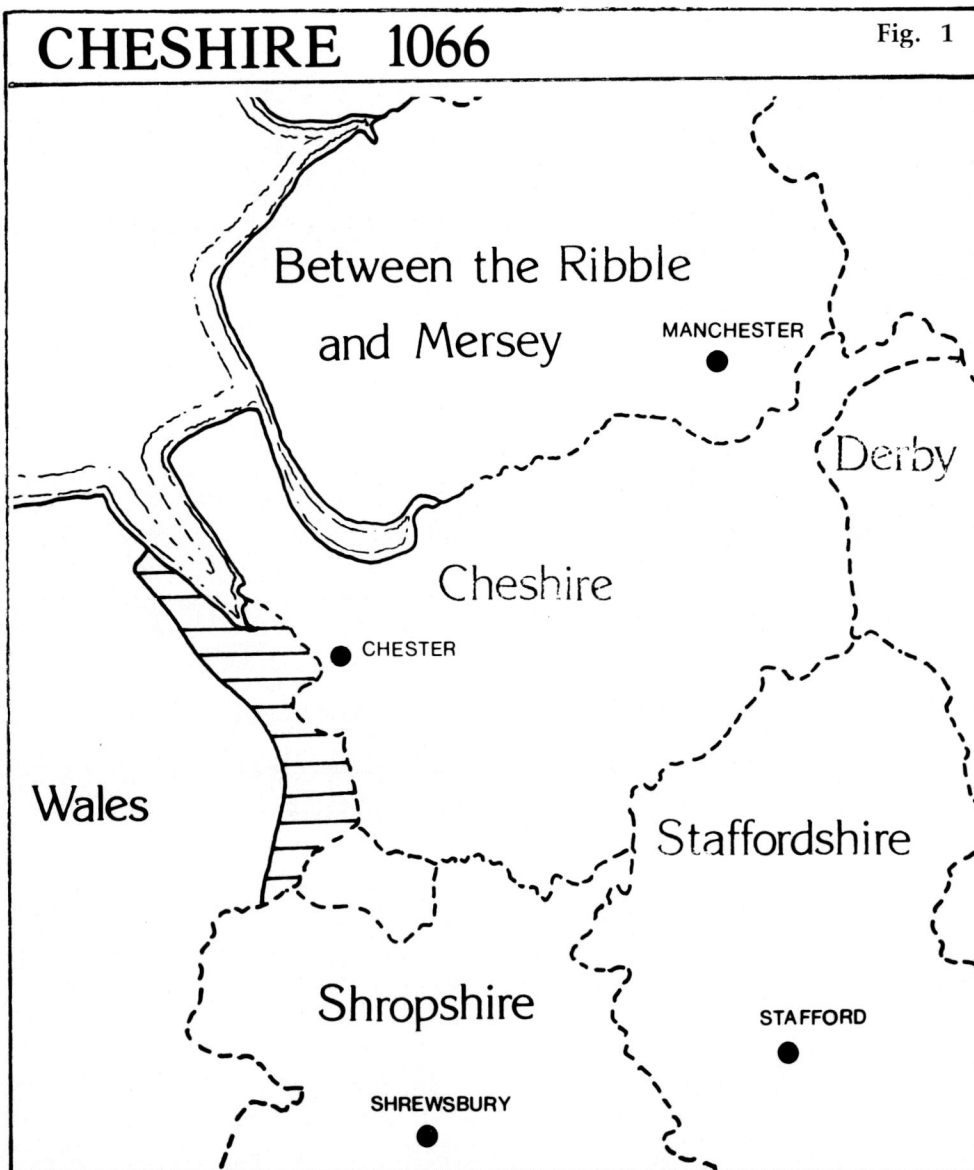

CHESHIRE 1066   Fig. 1

ANGLO-SAXON CHESHIRE

The establishment of the burhs

The burh was an Anglo-Saxon fortress designed to protect the whole community. Within Cheshire the building of four burhs has been recorded between 907 and 919.

In the late Anglo-Saxon period Cheshire, as a part of Mercia, was of great strategic importance. Its western fringe had long been a buffer against the Welsh and its northern boundary faced the Viking or Hiberno-Norse kingdom whose influence stretched from Dublin across to York.

The son of Alfred the Great of Wessex, Edward the Elder, made an alliance with the Mercians and took the offensive against the Viking kingdoms. He continued his father's policy of ensuring defence against the Vikings by building burhs. It was believed the Vikings disliked sieges and much preferred open battle.

The burhs had a wider purpose. In order to encourage trade, craftsmen and merchants were given town plots and markets and mints were established. The tolls from trading provided revenue which greatly increased the powers of Anglo-Saxon kings. The burh of Chester was established in 907 by Ethelred of Mercia. Although a small trading community was already in existence on the banks of the Dee the greater security helped it to become the most important centre in the North West of England.

As with other burhs outside Wessex Chester became the focus of the new administrative unit, the Shire or County. The Shire provided men to defend and repair the burh walls, which in Chester were the largely intact Roman fortifications (Fig. 2). The Domesday book entry for Chester states, "For the repair of the city wall the Shire Reeve (Sheriff) was wont to call up one man from each hide in the Shire".

The size of Cheshire may have been calculated from the length of the burh walls, and the number of men needed to defend them.

The burh established within the Iron Age Hill fort at Eddisbury in 913 by Aethelflaed, Ethelred's widow, was short-lived. Archaeological excavation in the 1930's revealed what may have been Anglo-Saxon reconstruction of the Iron Age ramparts.

In 915 Aethelflaed probably moved the Eddisbury garrison to Runcorn, where routes along the Mersey could be controlled. Nineteenth century developments destroyed all trace of this site, but records describe a defended area occupying a rocky promontory. The promontory was accessible by sea-going vessels and protected by a bank and a rock cut ditch.

Finally, there is Thelwall whose foundation is recorded in the Anglo-Saxon chronicle in the year 919. The entry states that Edward the Elder ordered a burh to be built, occupied and manned, but its location is still uncertain.

Only Chester remained an important centre in 1066, but this cannot have been the only defended site in the shire considering the threat from Wales.

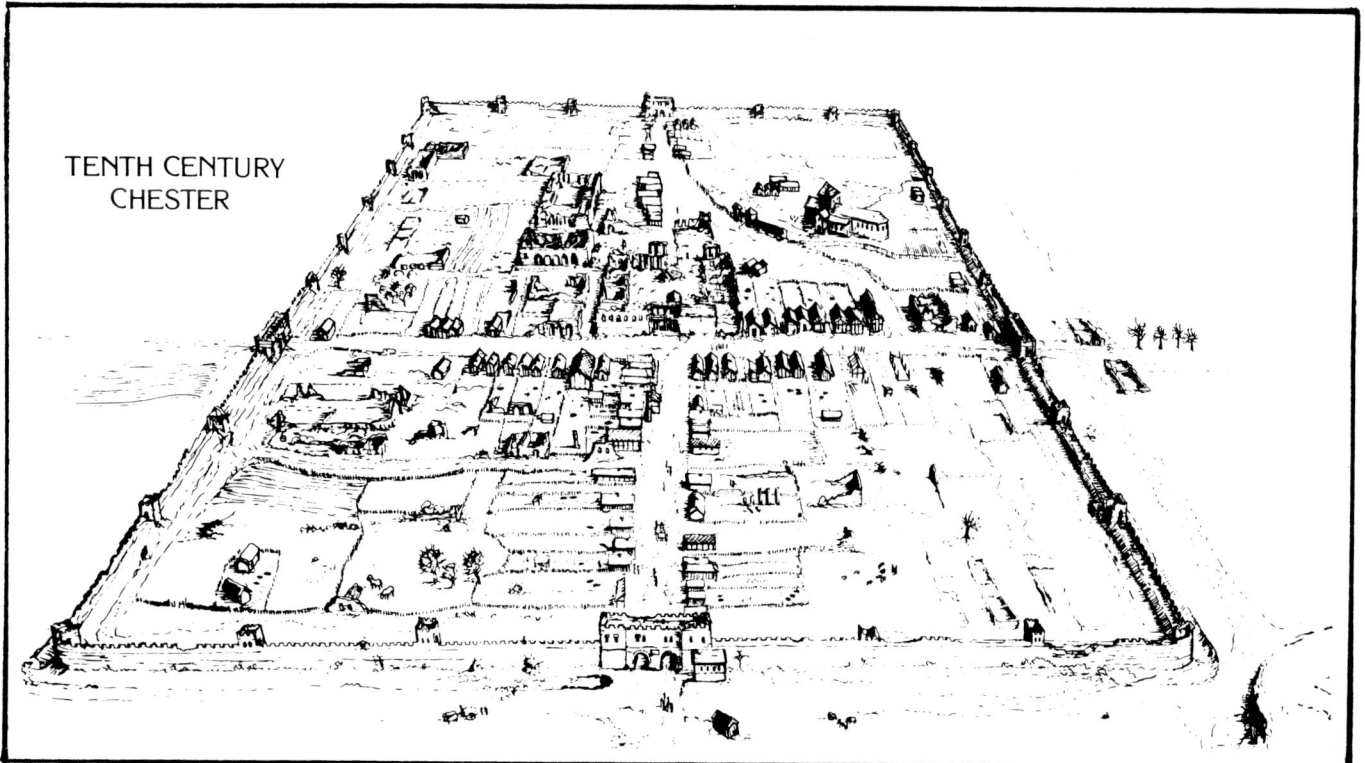

TENTH CENTURY CHESTER

Fig. 2 ANGLO-SAXON CHESTER
The Anglo-Saxon burh was established in the ruins of the Roman legionary fortress. Much of the Roman fabric was standing in the tenth century and the defences were serviceable. The Anglo-Saxon houses were aligned to the main Roman streets and after one thousand years of later modifications long sections of legionary fortress wall still stand to parapet level.

THE NORMANS

The Arrival of the Normans and the Devastation of Cheshire

William the Conqueror's victory over the last Saxon king at Hastings in 1066 only marked the beginning of a long struggle to gain complete control over the whole of England. Rebellions occurred throughout the country and by 1069 William's grip seemed tenuous. The Danes were attacking the east coast. The North of England and the West Country were in open revolt and a combined force of Welsh, Staffordshire, Shropshire and Cheshire men contributed towards the general decline into anarchy by storming Shrewsbury. William's conciliatory behaviour towards the English changed to one of ruthless repression. By 1070 the Normans had devastated much of Northern England including Cheshire where two-thirds of the manors were recorded as waste sixteen years later.

Chester suffered the destruction of half its houses and the imposition of the county's first Norman castle. Apart from those constructed in or near towns the early castles were not sited according to a systematic plan and by 1100 some five or six thousand had been built in England. Most were built by barons as private strongholds and were seen as symbols of the feudalism introduced by the Normans.

Earls, Barons and Knights

William's feudalism required that England should be divided into great estates granted on the basis of military service. The tenant of a large estate or "honor" was required to provide the king with a fixed number of knights. Gherbod was granted the earldom of Cheshire in 1069, but in the following year it was given to the King's nephew Hugh D'Avranches. Hugh granted out the Anglo-Saxon estates to his men whose descendants became the barons of the county. Hugh's men had each gathered a group of warriors including mounted soldiers or knights. The knights employed by the new Lords were not necessarily drawn from the upper classes or even Norman.

Knighthood did not seem to imply any social distinction in the eleventh century. Indeed, the knight of this time appears as a servant within a lord's household.

Some of a baron's household knights received land for their services. Among the obligations upon a knight holding land was "castle guard" which may have been performed upon a rota system. The land given was known as a "knight's fee" and it soon became hereditary. Clearly within a few years of the conquest it would be impracticable for the holder of a knight's fee to attend to the defence of his lord's castle in person. By the twelfth century it was common practice to gain discharge from military service by a cash payment, although in Cheshire there is no record of this practice before 1277.

The Privileged and Powerful Earls

The privileged Earls of Cheshire increased their power because of circumstance, ambition and a guarded loyalty to the Crown. They expanded their estates whilst other

NORMAN KNIGHT.
Norman Knights normally wore a mail hauberk which comprised a knee length coat of interlocking rings. The conical helmet was often provided with a strip to protect the nose and the kite shaped shield was designed to protect a horseman's leg. The spear was for throwing or thrusting and not used as a lance in a cavalry charge.

nobles fell from favour. Estates outside Cheshire provided the main source of wealth. In 1086 Earl Hugh received £200 in rents from Cheshire estates but £700 from all other areas.

The Earl of Cheshire, together with the Earls of Shropshire and Hereford were Marcher lords and therefore, expected to undertake a policy of conquest against the neighbouring Welsh. Testimony to the ferocity of the wars waged against the Welsh by the earls of Chester is found in this account recorded in the Chronicle of the Abbey of St Werburg at Chester for 1170 AD.

"In this year also Hugh, Earl of Chester, slew a multitude of Welshmen, near the bridge of Baldert, of whose heads one of the mounds at the hospital for the sick outside Chester is formed."

The special privileges granted gave them an authority which successive Earls of Chester alone managed to maintain. The administration of Cheshire was independent of Crown interference, and the sheriff, normally a Royal appointee, was chosen by the Earl. The

THE NORMAN EARLS 1071-1237

HUGH D'AVRANCHES 1071-1101
Gluttony, lust and love of hunting earned Hugh the titles "The Fat" and "Lupus" (the wolf). Savagery towards the Welsh and loyalty to three successive Kings gained him additional lands. With death impending he became a monk in St Werburghs, the monastic house which he had re-founded in 1091.

RICHARD OF THE WHITE SHIP 1101-1120
Earl Hugh's sole legitimate son. He inherited the earldom at the age of 7, so Henry I sent him to Normandy to receive his education. He was drowned when his ship sank in the English Channel along with Henry's only son, William.

RANULF I OF MESCHINES 1120-1129
Ranulf was a nephew of Hugh I and already powerful as Viscount of Bayeux in Normandy. He controlled much of Northern England and on inheriting Cheshire he demonstrated his loyalty to the crown by surrendering the Earldom of Carlisle.

RANULF II OF GERNONS 1129-1153
The son of Ranulf I he played a decisive role in the "anarchy", the power struggle between King Stephen and Matilda. Ranulf supported both sides at various stages emerging as the controller of one-third of England. His pledge of loyalty to Matilda's son Henry II gave him the lands of William Peveril of the Peak and his death was reputedly due to poisoning by the same William.

HUGH II OF GYFF YLLIOG 1153-1181
Hugh, Ranulf II's son initially supported Henry II's consolidation of Royal authority, but rebelled when he felt the policy was taken to excess. Although defeated he still kept his lands, as King Henry needed to foster good will having been blamed for the death of Thomas Becket, Archbishop of Canterbury.

RANULF III OF BLUNDEVILLE 1181-1232
Hugh's son, Ranulf III, once called a Dwarf, was the most powerful of all the Earls. He acquired Brittany and Richmond by his first marriage and supported King John in his struggle against the Barons in 1215. With the death of John he helped secure the throne for his young son Henry III in 1217. This loyalty earned him Lincoln and the Duchy of Lancaster and he was sufficiently powerful to resist both Royal and Papal demands for revenue from Cheshire lands.

Ranulf's determination to maintain his independence was emphasised by the alliance with his former enemies, the Welsh. He consolidated the alliance by marrying his nephew and heir John to Helen the Welsh prince's daughter. He then built Beeston castle in 1225 to protect both Cheshire and the route to Wales from England.

JOHN LE SCOT 1232-1237
He was the Earl of Huntingdon and also the nephew of the King of Scotland. John inherited Ranulf's Cheshire estates but Henry III resented the power of the Earldom and planned to secure Royal control after John's death which followed shortly, allegedly by poisoning.

Earl maintained his own court presided over by a justice, and his own financial administration supervised by a chamberlain. He also had the power to raise taxes and his barons were exempt from military service outside the county boundaries.

When King John ratified the Magna Carta in 1215, Ranulf III demonstrated his independence by issuing his own charter.

When the male line of earls ceased in 1237 the Crown took control of Cheshire, although it was held briefly by Simon de Montfort in the baronial wars of 1264/5. Since the time of Edward I it has been traditional for the eldest son of the monarch to carry the titles of Prince of Wales and Earl of Chester.

The separate county administration was continued. By the 14th century Cheshire, along with Durham and Lancashire, carried the title County Palatinate. Tudor and Stuart monarchs brought the Palatinate administration under closer supervision, and the last element of independence disappeared with the abolition of the Palatinate Courts in 1830. The county continued to bear the title Palatinate until local government reorganisation in 1974.

The Norman Castles

The early castles were built of earth and timber allowing rapid construction and in the event of retreat they could

Fig. 3 CASTLE ON THE BAYEUX TAPESTRY
A wooden structure is shown on top of an earth mound representing a castle in France.

Fig. 4 AN IMAGINATIVE RECONSTRUCTION OF A POST-CONQUEST VILLAGE
Motte and Bailey castles along the Welsh border were often built next to a parish church and dominated the surrounding Anglo-Saxon community.

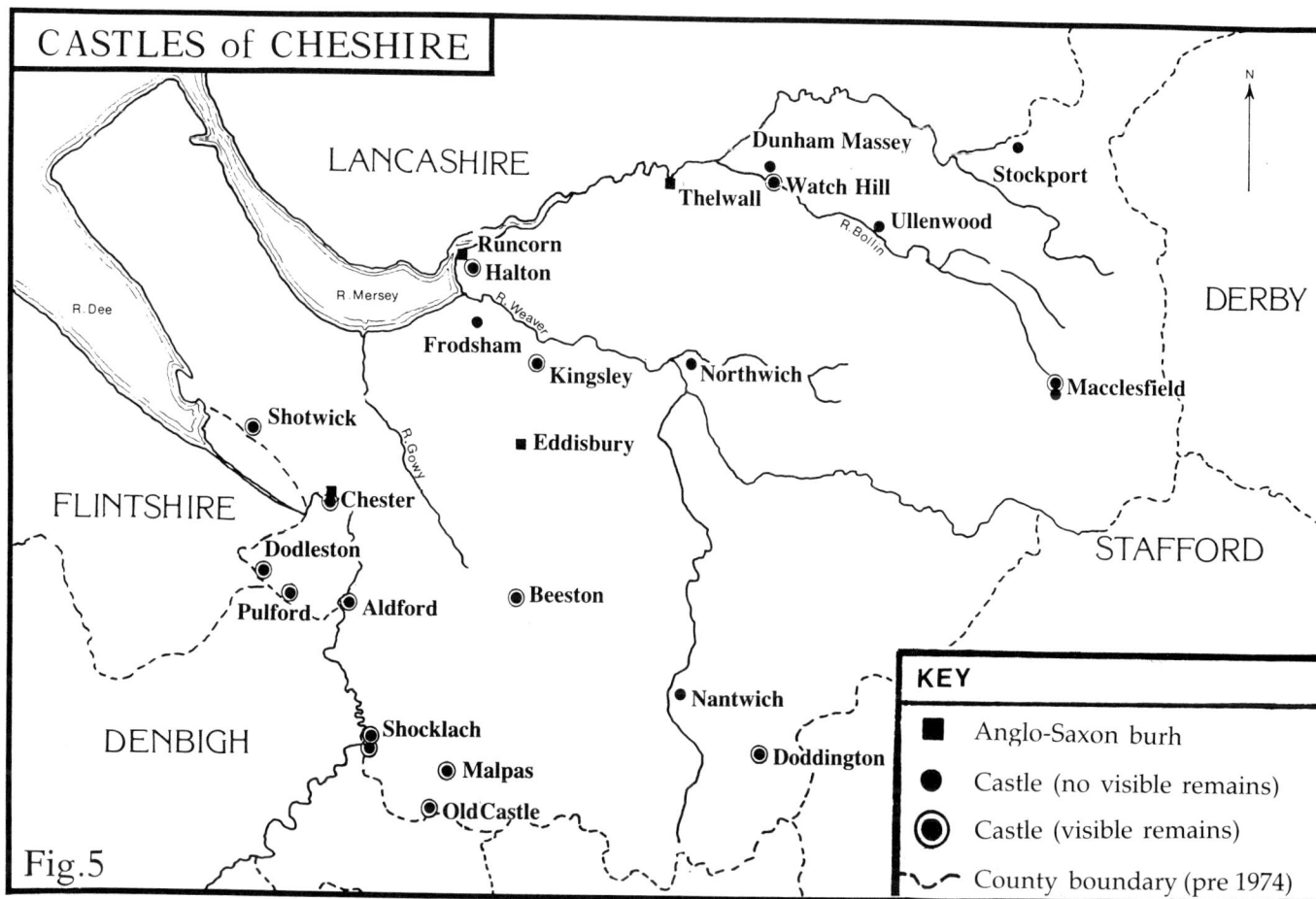

CASTLES of CHESHIRE

Fig.5

KEY
- ■ Anglo-Saxon burh
- ● Castle (no visible remains)
- ◉ Castle (visible remains)
- County boundary (pre 1974)

easily be rendered useless. Most comprised a conical mound, called a motte, surmounted by a wooden tower and palisade. Adjacent to the motte was the bailey which took the form of an enclosure containing workshops, stores, stables and living quarters. Both motte and bailey were surrounded by ditches. The Bayeux Tapestry suggests that the wooden structures of the motte and bailey castle were elaborate with carved decorations and bright paintwork (Fig 3).

The castles provided relatively secure bases for small cavalry units who patrolled the surrounding countryside. The distribution of the early castles in Cheshire reflected the concerns of the Earl and his barons. Since the barons had come into possession of established estates a number of castles may have been built on existing defences protecting the principal buildings of the Anglo-Saxon thegns. Many major Anglo-Saxon estates had acquired parish churches which were erected next to the thegn's chief residence. The Anglo-Saxon thegns had fortified private residences known as burgheats which, in some respects, were similar to the Norman castles.

They seem to have comprised an enclosure defended by a ditch and bank surmounted by a stockade with a gatehouse sometimes built of stone. The nearness of a number of Norman earthworks to ancient parish churches in Cheshire strongly suggests this sort of continuity (Fig 4).

The early castles can be put into three groups; those in the west of the county, along or near the River Dee; those of

the North having the appearance of a defensive line south of the Mersey; and the castles built at the important centres of Nantwich, Northwich and Macclesfield (Fig 5).

Castles of the West

Shotwick

Shotwick castle once stood on the shoreline of the Dee Estuary commanding a landing and ford. The construction of the first castle has been attributed to Hugh Lupus. Existing remains comprise a large flattened motte and a crescent shaped bailey of similar size. The motte must have been modified when it was provided with a stone ward and six towers. The ward contained at least two rectangular buildings and one of the towers was reputed to have been five storeys high. By the middle of the thirteenth century it had become one of the county's major strongholds and remained important until the conquest of Wales under Edward I. As a result the Dee estuary required less supervision but the castle was maintained well into the fourteenth century. Between 1325 and 1326 the mason Robert of Helpston worked on the fabric and in 1327 the land around became a Royal deer park. In 1331 Shotwick was included in a list of Royal castles to be inspected and repaired. It was still being attended to by the Crown in 1353 and the harbour was used to unload building materials for Chester castle. Towards the end of the fourteenth century it was granted out to Sir Hugh Calvely, thereafter the fabric began to deteriorate. In 1607 Camden noted that it was in ruins and much of the masonry remained until the middle of the eighteenth century when it was removed to make sea defences in the estuary.

Dodleston, Pulford and Aldford

South of Shotwick and West of the Dee stood Dodleston and Pulford. Dodleston castle sits next to an ancient parish church. The bailey was square and had water filled ditches whilst the motte is surrounded by a counterscarp slope. Nearby Pulford was considered worth a garrison as late as 1403 when Owen Glendower's Welsh troops threatened the county.

Substantial earthworks remain at Aldford. The motte was cut into by two boys in the 1950's to reveal what may have been the fragments of a shell keep. The motte is relatively large lying at the corner of a triangular bailey (Fig 6). The defences were being maintained as late as 1286 when the owner claimed that Hugh of Pulford had failed to repair two perches of hedging. The present parish church and churchyard are on the line of the bailey earthworks and probably mark the site of a pre-Norman structure. It is tempting to conclude that the Norman works at Dodleston, Pulford and Aldford covered or modified Anglo-Saxon defences.

Shocklack, Malpas and Oldcastle

A small complex of earthworks occur at Shocklack and appear to represent two stages in their development. The first castle was a motte and bailey and later a third defensive feature was built nearby in the form of an embanked plateau.

In common with Dodleston, Pulford and Aldford, Malpas castle is situated next to a parish church. The motte dominates the churchyard but there is no trace of a bailey, if it ever existed (Fig 7). It is assumed that Robert FitzHugh, son of Hugh Lupus, was responsible for its erection before 1100. The Domesday book records five knights at Malpas, then called "Depenbech", which must represent some of the garrison. Since Malpas was at the centre of a large parish and Anglo-Saxon estate its establishment must be linked to both the administrative importance of the settlements and its position on the Roman road leading to Chester.

Hugging the county boundary to the south is Oldcastle. There seem to be no historical references to throw any light on the origins or development of this site. It was investigated in the 1950's but dating evidence was not found. The remains lie near Wych brook on a spur in a river bend and comprise a motte defended by a series of ditches. It may have been an outpost of Malpas defending the valley of Wych brook.

Castles of the North
Frodsham

Frodsham was at the centre of a large Anglo-Saxon estate which belonged to Earl Edwin of Mercia in 1066. The lands were largely retained by the Norman Earls who built a

Fig. 6 ALDFORD
Aldford was at the centre of a large Anglo-Saxon estate. The Norman earthworks comprise a motte and a triangular bailey whose shape is marked by the lines of trees and the church yard.

castle which was later developed by the Crown. The ruins of Frodsham castle were finally demolished in 1727 to make way for Castle Park House and some of the remains were incorporated into the cellar.

Halton

The Norman castle at Halton was built upon a rocky outcrop overlooking the Mersey and South Lancashire (Fig. 8). It seems to have superseded the Anglo-Saxon stronghold at Runcorn whose position on the banks of the marshy estuary cannot have been attractive.

Halton was the centre of the barony of the hereditary constable of Chester who ranked second to the Earls. The first baron, Nigel, was granted land on both sides of the Mersey. His son, William, was responsible for leading the Earl's army into battle and held the title of "Marshal of the Earl's host". Five of his knights held land at Halton and include Odard, Geoffrey, Aethelhard, Humphrey and Hardwin.

The first substantial buildings were built in the late twelfth century by the fifth baron, Richard FitzEustace. He had married into the powerful Lacy family of Pontefract. John FitzRichard, the sixth baron, is believed to have established a ferry across the Mersey and founded the Cistercian monastery at Stanlow. After serving as governor in Ireland he went to the Crusades and died at the siege of Tyre in 1190.

John's descendant, Roger de Lacy, made a daring rescue of Earl Ranulf at the siege of Rhuddlan castle in 1216. He was supposed to have gathered a "tumult of fiddlers, players and debauched persons" from the streets of Chester to form an army. Their noise and appearance caused the Welsh to flee, so lifting the siege.

Towards the end of the thirteenth century the castle was formed around a court by the tenth baron, Henry. Henry was a close friend of Edward I and became the most powerful lord in England after his death.

In 1311 Halton passed by marriage to the House of Lancaster and by the late fourteenth century Halton was the favourite hunting lodge of the King's uncle, John of Gaunt, the Duke of Lancaster. John's son, Henry Bolingbroke, siezed the throne from Richard II and was crowned Henry IV in 1399. Many of Richard's followers came from Cheshire; he had stored his treasures at Beeston, and Henry executed twenty-six men from the county. Halton became part of Henry's Lancastrian inheritance and was administered separately from other crown possessions as it still is today.

The Crown modified and maintained Halton during the fifteenth century. A twin-towered gatehouse was built between 1450 and 1457 under the supervision of the King's master mason in Lancashire. The castle was still in use during the sixteenth century and went on to play an important role in the Civil War.

Today the little that remains lies behind the Castle Hotel, itself built on the site of the gatehouse from salvaged masonry.

Fig. 7 MALPAS
The motte at Malpas overlooks the churchyard and has a wide level plateau. There is no trace of a bailey and since it was at the centre of a large estate the surviving works seem rather modest.

Fig. 8 HALTON
This nineteenth century print illustrates the advantages of the site at Halton.

Dunham Massey

The estates of the Anglo-Saxon Lord Alfward had been acquired by Hamo of Masci in 1086. The centre of Hamo's estates, Dunham Massey, had been furnished with a castle whose remains probably lie beneath the present hall. The castle still functioned in 1323 as a dispute between the barons of Dunham and Nicholas of Audley regarding repairs show. Work carried out during the fourteenth century included plastering the hall and renewing joists in the chapel. The eighteenth century hall at Dunham was built by the 2nd Earl of Warrington whose family had gained the estates in the fifteenth century.

The Masseys also held the nearby motte at Watch Hill guarding a crossing over the River Bollin. It is possible that this castle was built during the rebellion against Henry II in 1173 as an outpost of the main stronghold at Dunham Massey.

Stockport

The position of Stockport's Norman motte and bailey has been established and the timberwork of the early fortification was probably replaced by stone walls before the end of the twelfth century. Stockport, together with Dunham Massey and the vanished Ullenwood, were held against the King in 1173. Although Stockport was in ruins by the sixteenth century the castle gaol was still standing.

Castles of Central and Eastern Cheshire
Nantwich and Northwich

The salt making centres of Nantwich and Northwich had early castles built to oversee the lucrative workings. Archaeological excavation has located the site of Nantwich's motte and bailey, but similar investigations failed to find Northwich's castle.

Macclesfield and Kingsley

At Macclesfield it is probable that the early motte lay in Castle field next to the Congleton road. Macclesfield was an important administrative centre and was in the possession of the Earl in 1086.

The small motte at Kingsley could easily be mistaken for a prehistoric burial mound. Its construction may be linked to the fondness the Norman Earls had for hunting in Delamere Forest.

Chester Castle

The foundation of Chester castle in 1070 occurred after the county had been devastated by William the Conqueror's forces. A natural bluff outside the walls of the Anglo-Saxon town was adapted to form a motte and this was accompanied by a bailey. It was the administrative centre of the earldom and a base for attacks on Wales. Sucessive earls developed the castle and by mid-twelfth century it was being rebuilt in stone and developed so as to have an inner and outer ward.

Between 1159 and 1160 £122-7s-6d was spent upon the castle, presumably for the construction of a curtain wall and square towers for the defence of the inner bailey. The surviving Agricola tower was the gateway to this part of the castle (Fig 9).

With the death of the last earl, John the Scot, in 1237 the earldom fell to the King who began building operations and restoration at Chester. In 1245 Henry III came to Chester with an army and the following year ordered the timber and earth defences of the outer bailey to be rebuilt in stone.

By 1251 £850 had been spent upon rebuilding the Earl's hall and exchequer chamber and in 1254 Henry made his son, Edward, Earl of Chester.

Henry III preferred French advisors and gradually alienated many of the barons whose estates lay principally in England. He lavished wealth on his relatives, on schemes of conquests in France and on the Church at the expense of his English subjects. Things came to a head in 1258 when the barons met at Oxford and took over the management of the country. Eventually the King resisted

Fig. 9 THE AGRICOLA TOWER
Most of the medieval castle was destroyed when Harrison's new prison was built in the years following 1784. Much of the inner ward, nevertheless, remains including the Agricola tower which was the original stone built gatehouse. The interior gateway remains, but the exit to the inner ward is not visible as Harrison had the tower refaced. Above the gate passage is a chapel entered by a stairway within the walls. The chapel roof is supported by stone vaulting adorned by moulded ribs springing from capitals decorated with floral designs.

and civil war ensued. The citizens of Chester, anticipating trouble, began to improve the defences of the city in March 1264. In the same year Henry was captured at Lewes and the leader of the barons, Simon de Montfort, summoned a Parliament whose composition marked a new development in English politics. By November Henry and his son Edward granted Simon de Montfort Chester castle and the county. William Zouche was replaced by Lucas of Taney as justiciary at Chester. In 1265 Edward escaped from the custody of Simon de Montfort and his followers besieged Lucas in Chester castle. In early August Simon was killed at the battle of Evesham and within a fortnight Lucas surrendered the castle after resisting for ten weeks.

Rebuilding in the late thirteenth century

Chester was a main base for Royal campaigns in North Wales, Ireland and Scotland. This stimulated a further rebuilding programme.

Between 1284 and 1291 £1,400-11s-7d was spent building new Royal apartments, stables and a chapel. The master of works, Richard the Engineer, was a rich citizen of Chester who held the manor of Belgrave and the mills along the River Dee.

Richard was not the only one to gain from Royal interest in the area as merchants flourished supplying provisions for troops and building workers. Chester was the gathering place of craftsmen brought from all over England to work upon the Edwardian castles of North Wales.

In 1293 the outer gatehouse of Chester castle was built; the plan was modified and when finished it comprised two drum towers and a gateway defended by two portcullises. Further work was done, including the decoration of the chapel in the outer ward and the adaptation of the chapel in the inner ward to take the treasure. There followed a fire in 1302 which damaged the Agricola tower and a number of buildings in the inner ward. Brother Thomas, the Plumber of Combermere Abbey, was employed to repair the roof of the Agricola tower. He was later to work on Beeston. The work was supervised by Richard the Engineer who was still working some forty years after building the stone wall of the outer bailey (Fig 10).

The Black Prince visited Chester twice and seems to have ensured that the fabric was maintained. Indeed, throughout the fourteenth century repairs and building continued with masons and carpenters being employed on a regular basis.

However, some administrative activities related to the earldom were taken out of the castle. In 1310 the court was moved to a hall outside the main gate and the exchequer followed in 1401.

The Royal interests in Cheshire meant a disproportionate number of Cheshire men served with the King. They had been accustomed to wars against the Welsh and were regarded as the most accomplished archers in the country. Cheshire archers played a leading part in the battles against the French at Crecy in 1346 and at Agincourt in 1415. Richard II used them as the core of his personal bodyguard and contemporaries described them as "arrogant insolent ruffians".

KEY
A Inner Ward
B Outer Ward
C Agricola Tower
D Gatehouse
E Hall
F Gatehouse
G Well

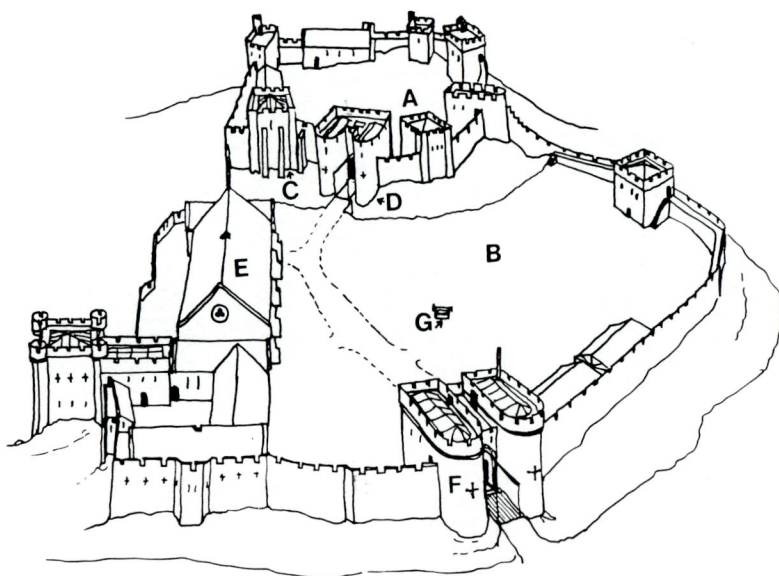

Fig. 10 CHESTER CASTLE IN THE EARLY FOURTEENTH CENTURY.
By 1300 the outer ward had been rebuilt in stone and both wards had twin towered gatehouses. It is probable that the interior of the outer ward contained numerous timber building and enclosures for animals.

Decay and Decline

During the fifteenth century the city of Chester began to decline, partly as a result of the silting up of the River Dee and perhaps because of the increased size of merchant vessels. The castle lost much of its former significance and fell into disrepair. During the reign of Henry VII an average of £25 a year was spent upon maintenance which, apparently, was not enough to preserve the structure. In 1511 some attempt at restoration was carried out, but by 1579 a major rebuilding programme was necessary (Fig 11).

The large thirteenth century hall was partly rebuilt and the old parliament building converted into the exchequer (Fig 12). Nevertheless, a heavy load of coal caused the castle bridge to collapse in 1585.

Apart from serving as a mustering point for soldiers en-route to Ireland and as a prison, the castle also provided lodging for the justices of the Assize courts. In 1590 they complained that their apartments and the accommodation for the prisoners let in the rain. In 1624 the justices noted that the only room suitable for prisoners was above the main gate and held both males and females. It would appear that the prisoners also amused themselves by throwing stones at the justices as they attempted to cross the ramshackle bridge. This resulted in the last major attempt at restoration before the Civil War. Some buildings were repaired and a new bridge built, but much of the castle was in ruins.

After the Civil War the castle remained in use as a garrison and prison.

Rebuilding and Restoration

In 1686/7 the garrison was provided with a new armoury in the inner bailey and a Keeper of Armoury was appointed. The Castle served as a supply base for campaigns in Ireland such as those of William II in the 1690's.

The threats posed by the Jacobite rebellions of 1715 and 1745 highlighted the crumbling state of the castle's defences. In 1745 the Lord Lieutenant, the Earl of Cholmondeley, obtained a plan for the building of four large bastions. The plan was the work of the military engineer Alex de Lavaix. It was never carried out, but some new emplacements for cannon were made.

The Castle housed prisoners from the Jacobite rebellions. In 1715 they were held in the outer gatehouse, many of them dying from the cold in a severe winter or from fever.

The prison was in vital need of improvements and the prison reformer, John Howard, had compared it to the Black Hole of Calcutta. Thomas Harrison (1744-1829) was commissioned in 1785 to design new buildings, and he was to work on Chester's North gate, the Grosvenor Bridge and the Lyceum in Liverpool. He built in the Greek Revival style with a large Doric gateway fronting the extended area of the castle. Acts of Parliament of 1788 and 1807 allowed the demolition of much of the medieval castle.

On the north side of the parade ground (now used as a car park) is the central building of the scheme, containing the main Shire Hall and the new court room. The two wings

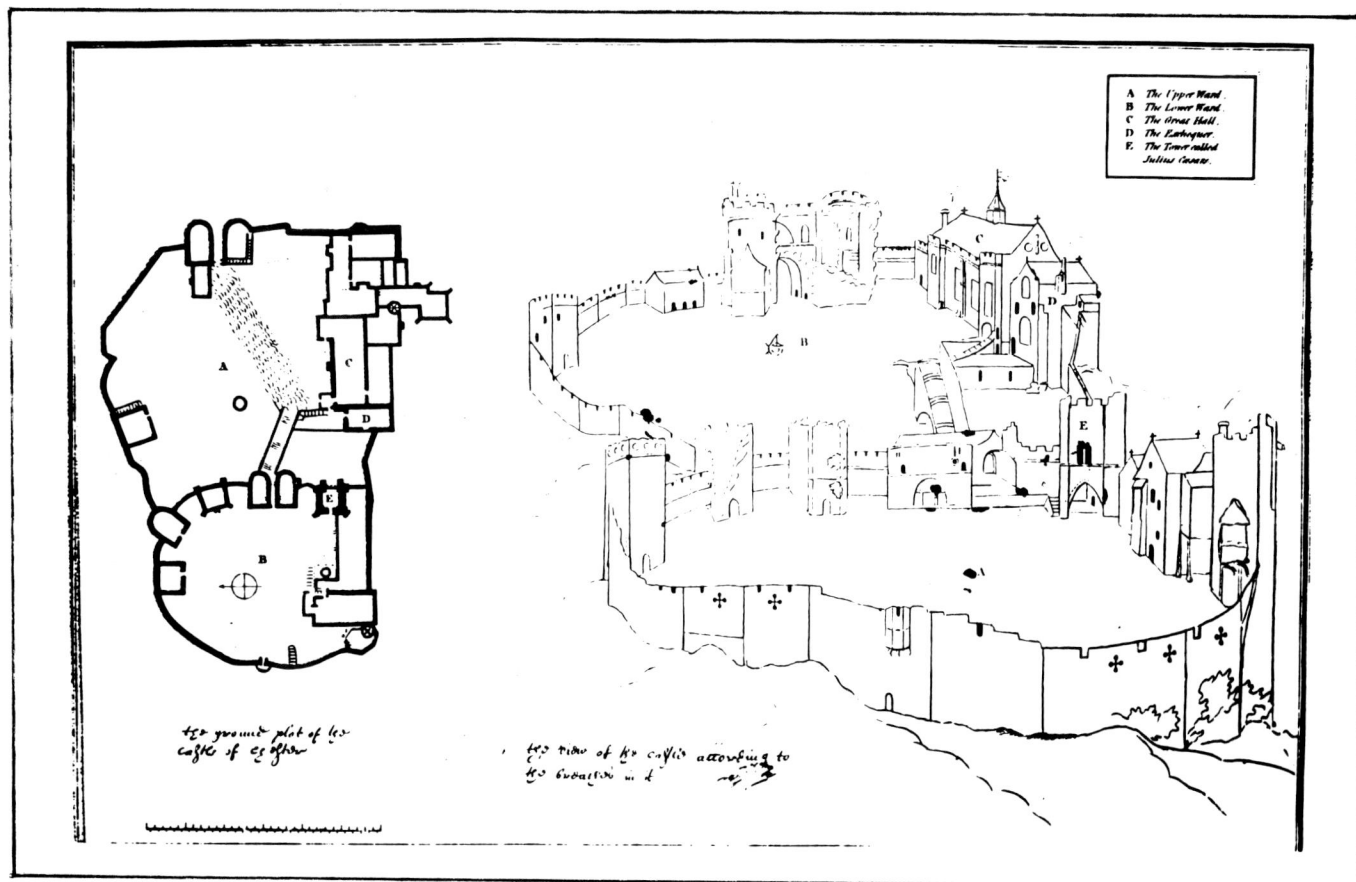

Fig. 11 CHESTER CASTLE IN THE SIXTEENTH CENTURY.
The sketch and plan is thought to have been drawn in the sixteenth century. It shows that the defences had been allowed to fall into decay.

Fig. 12 CHESTER CASTLE HALL AND EXCHEQUER.
This print shows the medieval Hall and Exchequer before its demolition.

Fig. 13 AERIAL PHOTOGRAPH OF CHESTER CASTLE.
The form of the inner ward can be seen in the bottom left of the photograph.

adjacent to the main block housed an armoury, barracks and exchequer court. The northern wing now houses the military museum and the southern wing was later converted into officers' quarters. Behind the main block the new model prison was built but this was taken over by the government in 1877 and later demolished. The County Council's administrative centre, County Hall, was built on its site before the 2nd World War.

The Castle continued to remain outside the jurisdiction of the city until local government reorganisation in 1974.

The medieval sections which have survived include the Agricola Tower, refaced by Thomas Harrison, the Flag Tower, the Half Moon Tower and part of the curtain wall of the inner bailey (Fig 13).

Chester City Walls

The castle of Chester lay outside the town walls of 1086 in the parish of St Mary which was part of the hundred of Broxton. It was built within the township of Gloverstone which retained its independence from Chester's civic government after the walls were extended to enclose the castle in the early twelfth century. It was to remain free from the mayor's jurisdiction for many centuries with the area outside the castle walls supporting taverns and brothels .

When Chester's walls were modified the Roman south and west walls were demolished and some of the masonry was used to build the new circuit. The north and east sections of the Roman walls were refurbished and incorporated in the re-planned defences.

Eastgate, the main entrance to the medieval town, was shown to have contained substantial Roman work when demolished in 1769 (Fig 14). Following the wall north there used to be a postern called Kaleyard gate nearby the Saddlers tower. The north eastern corner possessed the medieval Phoenix tower, later called King Charles' tower.

The medieval Northgate survived until 1808 and had been used as a prison. Further west stands Morgan's mount set above the Roman north western corner tower. Between Morgan's mount and the Water Tower stood two medieval towers called Dille's and Bonewaldethorne's. The north western corner of the wall has a spur connecting the Water Tower to the defences. The spur and tower were built between 1322 and 1325 under the guidance of Roger Helpston and were designed to protect the harbour of Chester.

To the south stood Watergate which gave access to the harbour but its medieval structure was demolished in 1788. After the Watergate the walls ran south and encompassed the castle. Following the River Dee the wall ran to Bridgegate. Once again the medieval gate was removed in the eighteenth century, together with the neighbouring Shipgate. Proceeding northwards two small bastions were sited before the Wolf Gate, later superseded by New Gate. Adjacent to Wolf Gate was

CASTLEBUILDING: DEVELOPMENTS

The early motte and bailey castles of the post-conquest period were cheap and easy to build but within a short time were being rebuilt in stone. Often a curtain wall was built around the bailey containing a keep which was rarely built upon a motte as they failed to provide a firm foundation. The keep became the strongest part of the castle comprising a massive turreted tower. In 1215 King John's forces did destroy the corner turret of Rochester's keep but the defenders continued to resist behind an internal dividing wall (A). Nevertheless, in some cases the motte was surrounded by a stone wall called a shell keep as at Restormel (B).

A ROCHESTER CASTLE

B

Orford's polygonal keep of the twelfth century shows an attempt to avoid the problems presented by the vulnerable corners of the traditional rectangular keep (C). However, the keep began to be abandoned towards the end of the twelfth century in favour of walled enclosures defended by projecting towers. The concept of projecting towers was not new as Roman ruins throughout the country demonstrate (D).

C

D

The weakest part of the castle was the gate and by the early thirteenth century powerful gatehouses had replaced the keep as the principal element of the defences. Beeston was one of the first castles in the country to have such a gate defended by solid "D" shaped towers (E).

Some of the most sophisticated medieval fortifications were the concentric castles built towards the end of the thirteenth century. North Wales has a number of concentric castles built for Edward I including Rhuddlan, Harlech and Beaumaris (F).

E

F

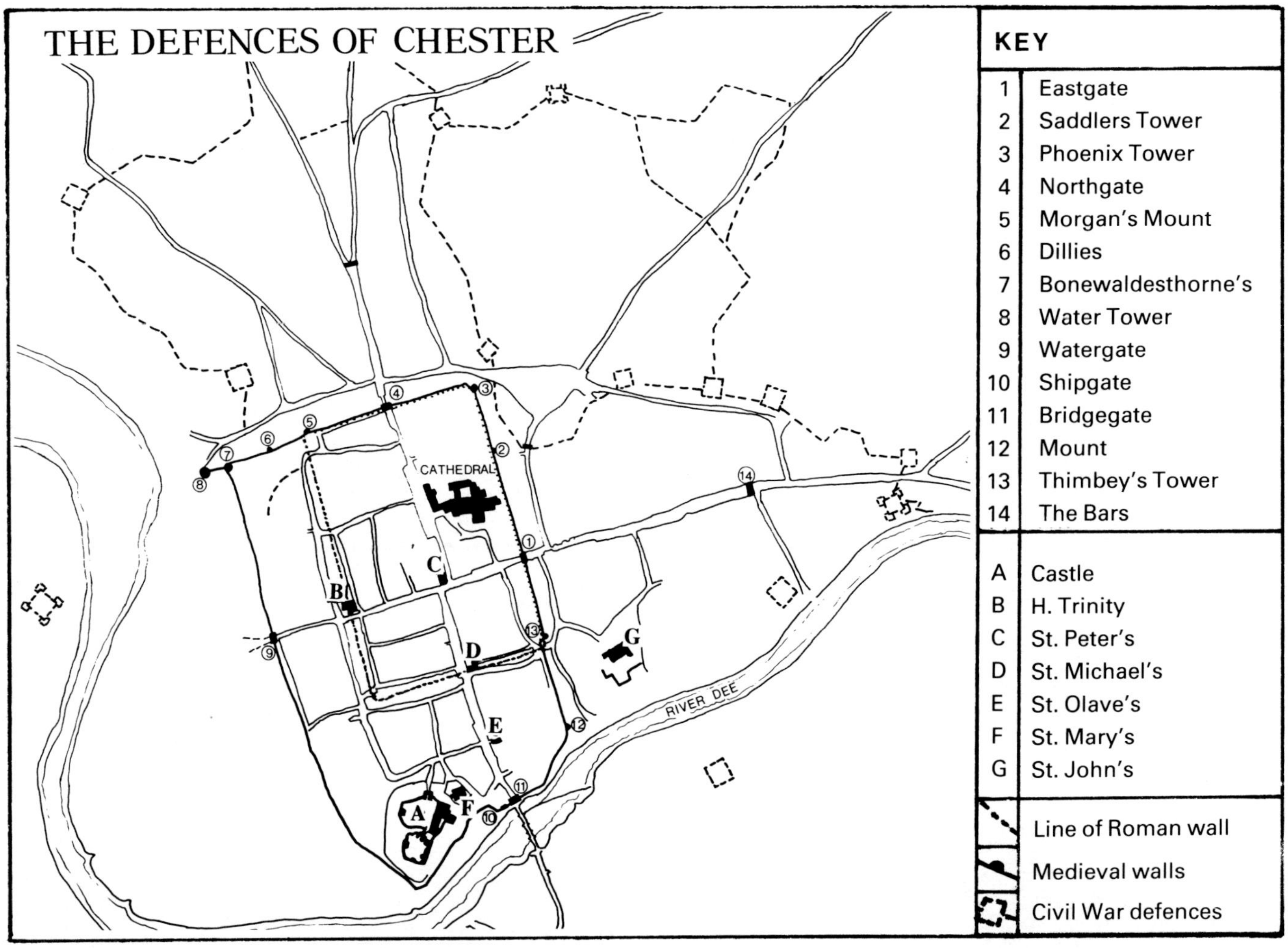
THE DEFENCES OF CHESTER
CATHEDRAL
RIVER DEE
KEY
1 Eastgate
2 Saddlers Tower
3 Phoenix Tower
4 Northgate
5 Morgan's Mount
6 Dillies
7 Bonewaldesthorne's
8 Water Tower
9 Watergate
10 Shipgate
11 Bridgegate
12 Mount
13 Thimbey's Tower
14 The Bars
A Castle
B H. Trinity
C St. Peter's
D St. Michael's
E St. Olave's
F St. Mary's
G St. John's
Line of Roman wall
Medieval walls
Civil War defences

Fig. 14 EASTGATE. CHESTER
Eastgate was demolished in 1769 and was shown to have contained a substantial proportion of Roman masonry.

Thimbleby's tower bolstering the defences that ran to Eastgate.

During the Civil War the suburbs were protected by earthen banks and forts but, the defenders were required to withdraw behind the medieval walls, which successfully withstood numerous attacks. Restoration work was undertaken in the 18th and 19th centuries in order to provide a scenic footpath around the city.

Beeston Castle

Beeston castle stands upon a sandstone outcrop commanding the Tarporley Gap. Wales, Merseyside, the Pennines and the wide Cheshire plain can be seen from the summit. The site was fortified by the Bronze Age and has seen intermittent periods of occupation ever since.

In 1225 the sixth Earl of Cheshire, Ranulf de Blundeville, ordered the building of the castle and in order to pay for the work he levied a tax upon all those passing through his lands (Fig 15).

Ranulf's Welsh alliance probably led the crown to view the castle as a threat and within five years of his death it became Crown property. In 1241 Henry III used Beeston to contain prisoners from his Welsh campaign and soon after the defences were refurbished.

When the castle was briefly held by the supporters of

Fig. 15 RECONSTRUCTION OF BEESTON'S INNER WARD IN 1225.
This conjectural reconstruction shows the inner ward gatehouse soon after its completion.

Simon de Montfort their alliance with the Welsh once again raised the possibility of the fortress serving as a defence for Wales rather than England. In the event Beeston surrendered to Prince Edward without a struggle.

Edward I's conquest of Wales involved the construction of ten castles. Beeston was then modified to bring it up to the new defensive standards as it was viewed as part of a second line of defence against the Welsh (Fig 16). Richard the Engineer was employed to do the work in 1303. Comprehensive accounts survive to give some insight into the activities involved in the reconstruction (Fig 17). Warrin the mason and twenty-four craftsmen were engaged to build a stone causeway across the moat and modify the inner-ward gatehouse to take a drawbridge. The towers of the inner ward had their pitched timber roofing removed so that the walls could be raised and crenellated. The roofs were flattened and protected with lead sheeting by Thomas the Plumber, a monk of Combermere Abbey (Fig 18).

The carpenters under Hugh of Dymoke as part of their work erected a crane to lift heavy timber into the inner bailey. A smith was engaged to set up a forge on the site for the manufacture of hinges, locks, keys and tools required by the masons and carpenters.

Repairs on a smaller scale were carried out in the years 1312, 1325 and 1358, paralleling work on the Welsh castles.

Castles normally had surprisingly small garrisons and Beeston was no exception having a governor, two squires and six bowmen in 1312. Times of conflict saw a rapid increase of numbers and Beeston was defended by a hundred men in order to guard Richard II's treasure and jewels, valued at 200,000 marks. Richard had considered Beeston a secure place during his dispute with Henry Bolingbroke, the Duke of Lancaster, but it was surrendered as soon as his forces arrived. The belief that the treasure remained hidden in the castle persisted for many centuries but, unfortunately it appears that Bolingbroke took it to Chester.

At the conclusion of the Baronial Wars of the fifteenth century the castle fell into disrepair. In 1502 the keeper was obliged to remind the Crown to pay his wages and by the end of the sixteenth century it had been sold to Sir

Fig. 16. BEESTON CASTLE IN THE EARLY FOURTEENTH CENTURY
After the reconstruction of the early fourteenth century Beeston became an even more formidable stronghold.

Fig. 17 CROSS SECTION THROUGH THE GATEHOUSE OF THE INNER WARD AT BEESTON.
The Gatehouse of the inner ward was modified in 1304 being provided with a portcullis and a drawbridge possibly raised by ropes or chains rather than a counterbalance.

Fig. 18 VIEW OF GATEHOUSE AT BEESTON FROM THE INTERIOR OF THE INNER WARD
Access to the upper floor of the gatehouse was by an outside stairway.

THE THIRTEENTH CENTURY KNIGHT.
By the early thirteenth century the surcoat was in general use. The "great helm" suit of mail and the "flat iron" shield protected the body.

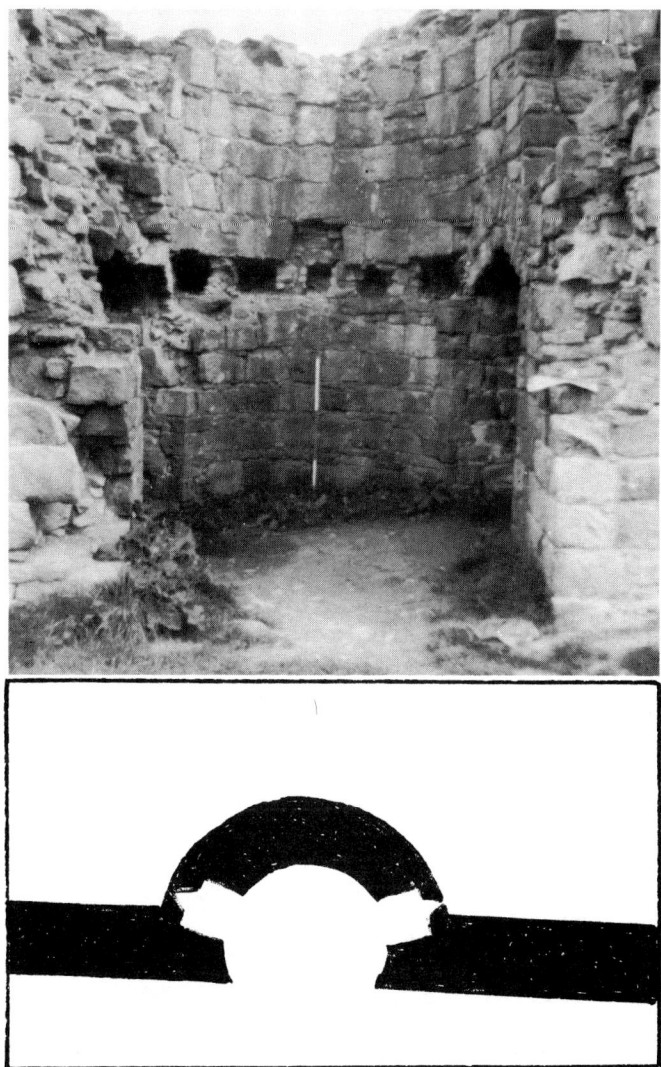

Fig. 19 OPEN BACKED TOWER ALONG THE LINE OF THE CURTAIN WALL, BEESTON
The open back denied cover to any attacker who gained access to the inner ward.

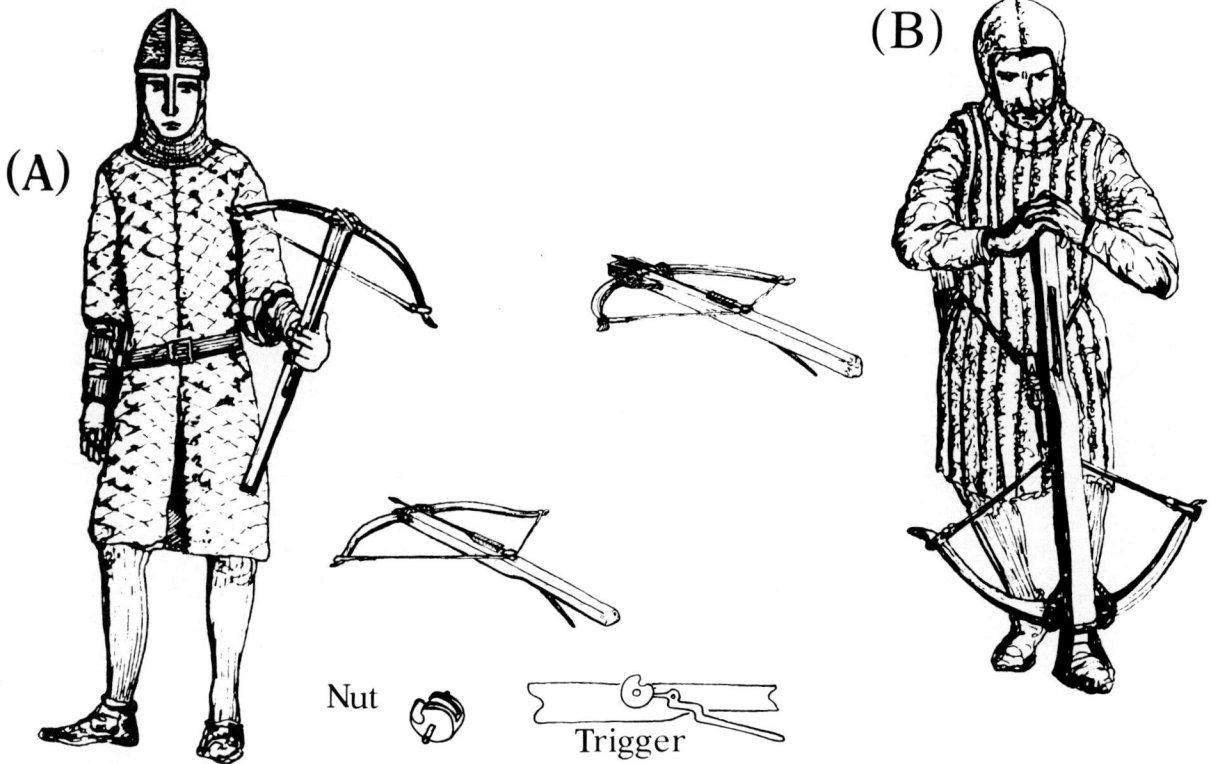

Nut

Trigger

CROSSBOWS.

In the years after the Norman Conquest the crossbow became more sophisticated and increasingly important. The Bayeux Tapestry does not show crossbowmen but it appears a simple form was in use (A). By the thirteenth century they had become more powerful with the use of a hook and stirrup to stretch the cord (B).

SIEGE WARFARE

After the death of Simon de Montfort in 1265 Chester castle surrendered to the King's forces; however Kenilworth castle continued to resist. In 1266 Kenilworth was besieged by Henry III who employed nine stone throwing engines (A) (B) to bombard the defences day and night. Two belfries (C) were then built in order to overlook the walls and shower arrows onto the defenders. They were never deployed against the walls as the stone throwing engines within the castle destroyed both. A prolonged duel between the engines ensued resulting in the destruction of those within the castle. At the same time barges were brought from Chester for a proposed water-borne assault across the lake which defended the south and west sides of Kenilworth. After six months the attack across the lake had not taken place and the King was close to financial ruin. Fortunately by this time the garrison had run out of food and came to terms.

A

MANGONEL

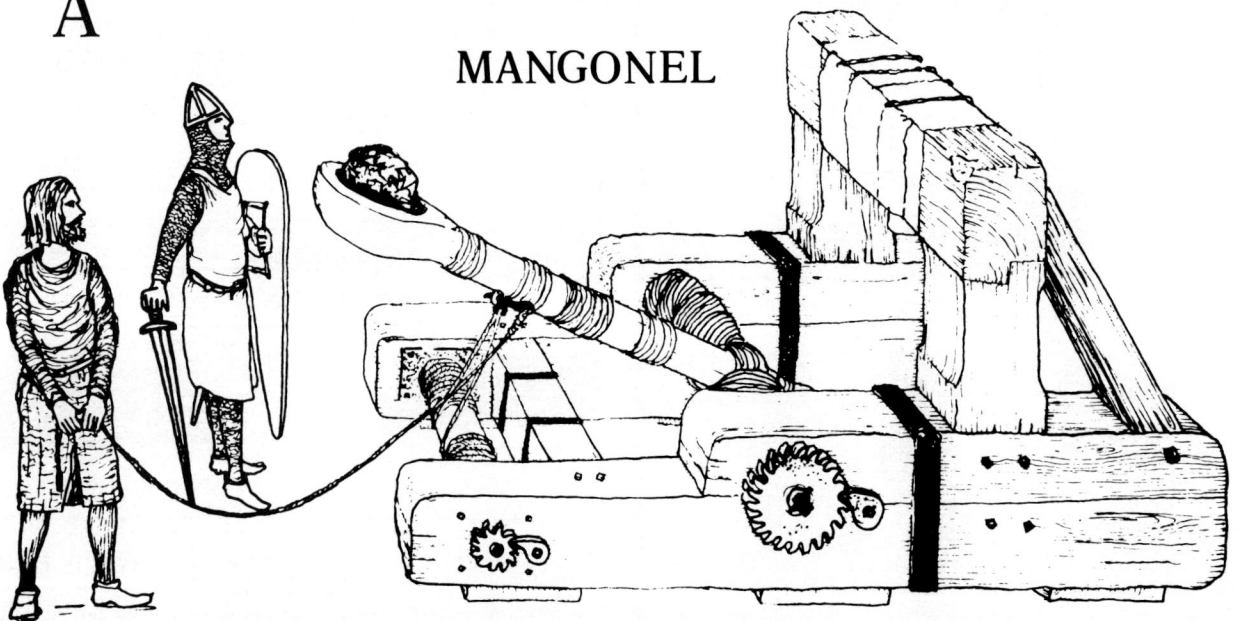

SIEGE WARFARE

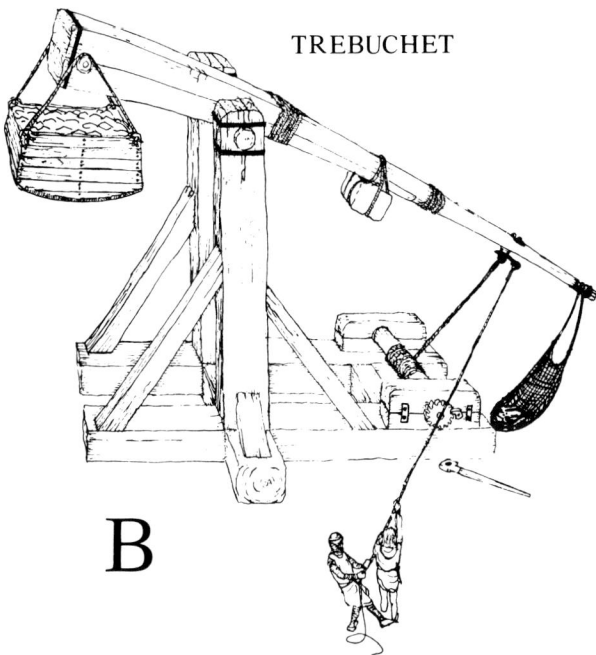

TREBUCHET

B

C

The example of Kenilworth demonstrated that the ability of castles to withstand a siege largely depended upon their capacity to provide fresh water and store provisions. Despite the array of equipment that a powerful attacker could bring against a castle very few fell in the face of direct assault. Treachery, subterfuge, thirst and starvation accounted for the fall of most castles. Nevertheless attackers continued to use rams (D), bores (E) and undermining (F), apart from those methods cited above, in attempts to force an entrance.

D

E

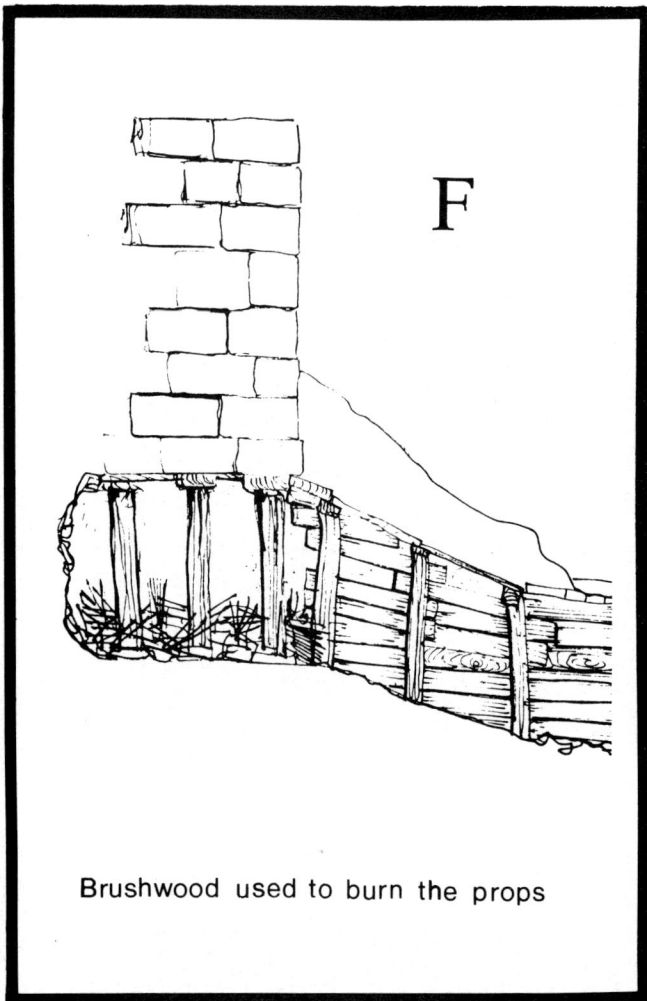

Brushwood used to burn the props

KNIGHT OF THE EARLY 14th CENTURY
By the 14th century plates of metal or hardened leather were being worn over the mail.

Hugh Beeston. Some of his elderly relatives were housed in the sixteenth century addition to the gatehouse of the outer ward. By the early seventeenth century the decayed castle was becoming a tourist attraction. It had never been tested by siege but it was still to play an important role as a stonghold.

The Castle Grounds

Unlike the other Cheshire castles the principal elements of Beeston's medieval stone defences can still be seen. The turretted entrance to the castle and the surrounding wall were built by the 19th century owners, the Lords of Tollemache, to blend in with their home, Peckforton castle, on the ridge opposite. A museum is housed inside the entrance and from here the path leads to the medieval outer ward.

The Outer Ward

The walls of the outer ward enclose 9.5 acres (3.8 hectares) and may have been built on Iron Age defences. There is no trace of medieval building, except for a well near to the curtain wall on the south side.

Much of the wall has disappeared due to quarrying in the 18th and 19th centuries, but the seven medieval towers and the gatehouse survive. The towers were originally two-storeyed with fighting platforms. Some still contain arrow slits which allowed bowmen to cover the approaches to the curtain wall and the adjoining towers.

All the towers except one were open at the back denying cover to any attackers who had gained access (Fig 19). Rapid movement along the curtain wall was allowed by stairways giving access to wall-walks and to the tops of the towers.

The Inner Ward

The inner ward was defended by a deep moat, a twin-towered gatehouse and three towers. Strong gatehouses were developed in the 13th century as an alternative to keeps or central towers. On the north western side a low wall was sufficient due to the steep precipice.

The moat was cut into the sandstone which was used in the building of the castle. Such moats were built principally to prevent siege towers and battering rams being used against the walls. At first the moat was crossed by a wooden bridge, but in the alterations of 1303/4 it was replaced by a stone causeway, connected to the gatehouse by a drawbridge (Fig 20). The gateway was protected by two sets of doors and a portcullis.

The remaining fragments of curtain wall still possess some merlons, embrasures and sockets for hoardings along the south east corner of the wall (Fig 21). The interior of the inner ward was intended to contain various buildings to serve the garrison but the original scheme was never completed. The Cheshire Chamberlain's accounts of 1241/2 suggests some wooden buildings within the inner ward including barracks, an armoury and a granary. The gatehouse is known to have provided spartan accommodation for the constable.

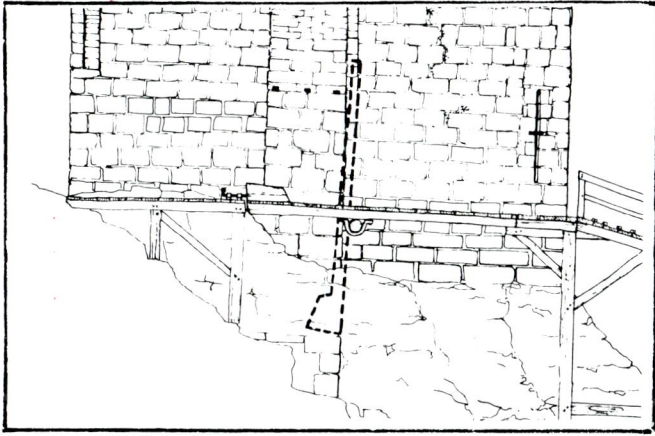

Fig. 20 DRAWBRIDGE SYSTEM BEFORE RECONSTRUCTION IN 1303/4.
The section shows the gatehouse of the inner ward at Beeston. Sockets in the stonework suggest that the original drawbridge was raised with the aid of a counterbalance.

Fig. 21 THE HOARDINGS.
At Beeston the sockets or putlogs can still be seen along the curtain wall of the inner bailey which supported hoardings. The sketch restores the hoardings and shows how they were used to allow missiles to be thrown at attackers below.

Fig. 22 BEESTON CASTLE DURING THE CIVIL WAR.
Despite its loss by a surprise attack Beeston proved a strong defensive position when manned by an alert garrison.

One of the most impressive engineering works at Beeston is the well of the inner ward hewn to a depth of 370 feet (11.2 metres).

The castle was acquired by the then Ministry of Public Buildings and Works in 1959. Developments have included the construction of a bridge across the ditch leading to the inner ward. Archaeological excavations have shown that the site has been occupied since the New Stone Age.

The Later Castles

Macclesfield and Doddington

Three other medieval fortified places deserve mention in this work, two in Macclesfield and that at Doddington. By the fifteenth century there were two fortified places in Macclesfield. In 1398 the clerk, John of Macclesfield, applied for a licence to crenellate his mansion and towards the end of the fifteenth century the Duke of Buckingham built a large fortified manor. By all accounts the "castle" built by the Duke was large and spectacular and some fragments remain.

At Doddington John de Delves received a licence to crenellate in 1405. The building has been described as a two storey keep with battlements and turrets.

At Brimstage the unfortified hall has an adjoining tower containing a spiral staircase. It probably dates from the early fifteenth century and seems to have served no military function.

The Gothic Revival

The gothic revival of the 19th century saw the resurrection of medieval military architecture. Bolesworth, built in 1830 by William Coe, is a two-storeyed building both turretted and castellated. Cholmondeley castle is also a 19th century castellated structure, built on the site of a 16th century house itself remodelled in the 18th century. Leasowe, built in 1593 by the Earl of Derby, was given a castellated front in 1818.

A complete 19th century replica of a medieval castle is found at Peckforton, on the ridge opposite Beeston. It has a moat, an inner and outer ward, a gatehouse and a great hall. Built in 1844 by the Victorian architect Anthony Salvin it represents the ultimate attempt to recreate a medieval castle.

Cheshire Castles in the English Civil War

Cheshire's medieval fortifications saw active service for the last time in the first English Civil War.

One of the main reasons for the outbreak of the civil war was King Charles I's (1625-1649) belief in absolute monarchy. "Princes are not bound to give account of their

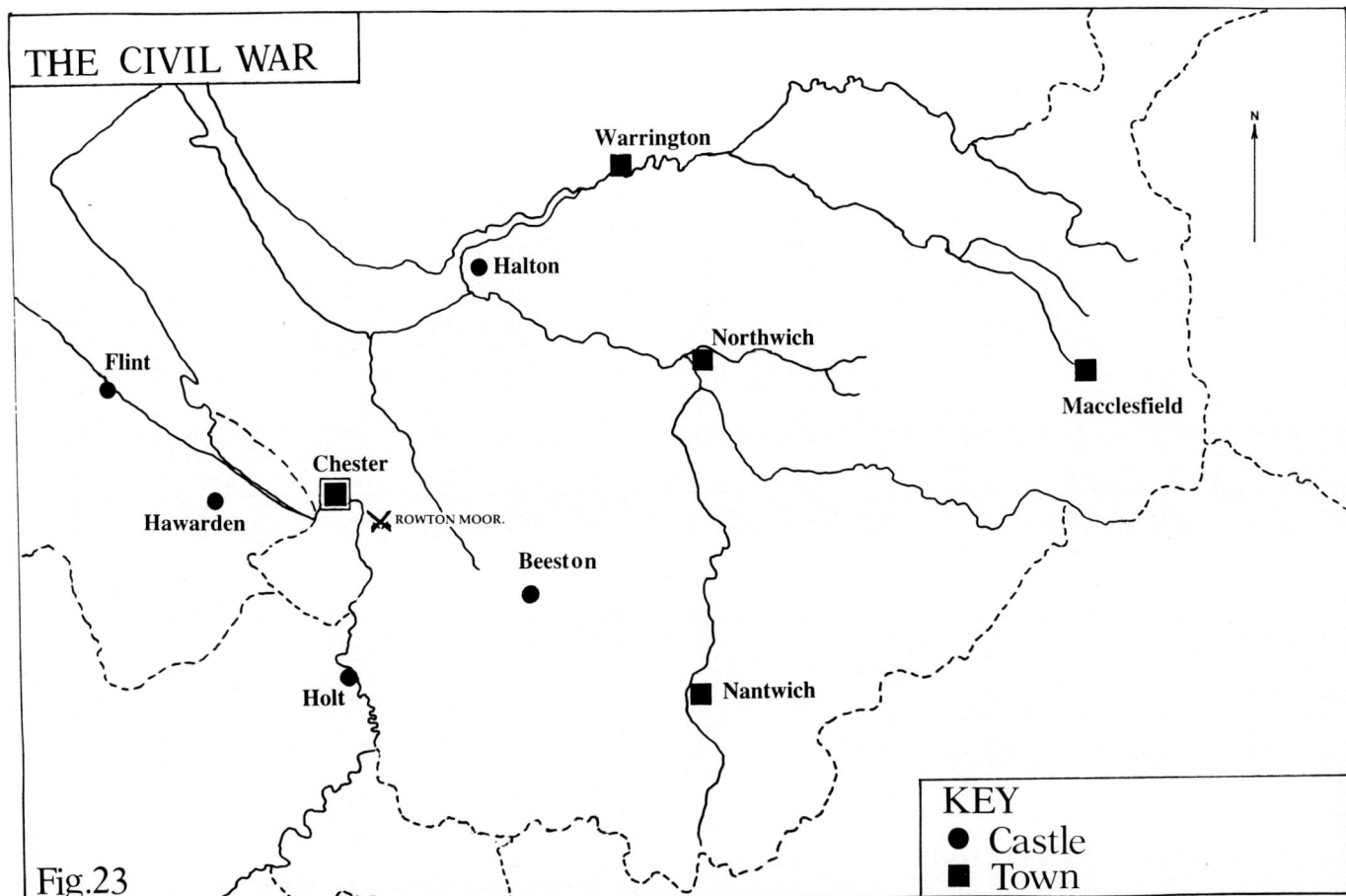

Fig.23

actions but to God alone." He was opposed by Parliament where many of the landed gentry and mercantile classes demanded a greater say in policy making.

At the beginning of the war the areas of Parliamentary support were commercially prosperous, and the centres of opposition to High Church Anglicanism. This gave Parliament the control of London, the south and the east and many leading ports. The King held most support in the north, Wales and the west, generally the less developed parts of the country.

No side was dominant in the early stages. With the battles of Marston Moor (1644) and Naseby (1645), the tide turned for Parliament who had the more astute commanders, including Fairfax and Cromwell.

The divisions of the Civil War were reflected within Cheshire. Two of Daniel of Over Tabley's sons died fighting for the King and two fought for Parliament. It appears that the loyalties of many combatants were irresolute as defeated troops frequently joined the victorious side. After the battle of Nantwich many Royalist troops defected to the Parliamentarian army. A desire for self-preservation led William Davenport of Bramhall Hall to send recruits to a Royal muster and £100 to Parliament.

The obsolete and dilapidated defences in Cheshire and the Welsh hinterlands were pressed into service. Chester, Hawarden and Holt controlled the routes to Royalist North Wales. Halton commanded a crossing over the River Mersey, and Beeston Castle served as a vantage point overlooking central Cheshire. Chester enjoyed an additional importance as its outports along the Dee could receive troops and supplies from Ireland.

King Charles rallied support in Chester in September 1642 after the Parliamentary commander and county M.P. Sir William Brereton had failed to raise a militia for Parliament. The Royalists controlled Chester and the majority of the county in the early stages of the war and were largely responsible for the construction of defensive works.

Preparations for war at Chester

The Royalist military governor at Chester, Sir Nicholas Byron, appointed in 1643, was responsible for general military strategy and after his capture at Ellesmere in 1644 he was succeeded by his nephew Lord John Byron. The main fighting force was the militia under Colonel Francis Gamul which was strengthened in 1642 with 300 musketeers and supplemented in 1643 with a general call to arms of citizens aged 16 to 60. The appointment of Byron saw the rapid improvement of the city's defences. The north and east suburbs were protected by earthen banks, bastions for cannon and mounts for musketeers. The gates were improved and drawbridges added to the Northgate, Eastgate, the Bridgegate and the Castle. Eastgate was later blocked. The Castle was administered separately by a High Constable and it remained as a prison. State papers of 1642 show it was reinforced with 12 great guns, and in 1643 it was stockpiled with 3 years food supply.

The Events of 1643

In 1643 Cheshire assumed greater prominence in the war.

The Royalists had made a treaty with rebels in Ireland which freed the King's Irish army for service in England and Wales. These reinforcements were needed as the Parliamentarians mounted a new offensive, crossing into Wales and occupying Hawarden in order to isolate Chester. In February a small Parliamentary detachment occupied the ruins of Beeston castle. The garrison was quartered in the large outer ward where they repaired the walls with earthen banks. In May Halton castle came under threat following the Parliamentary victory at Warrington. Ditches and mounts were dug around the castle by the beseiging army, and with supplies exhausted the Royalist commander, Captain Walter Primrose, surrendered to the Parliamentarian, Colonel Brereton, in July 1643. Brereton mounted an attack on Chester in the same month, lasting 3 days.

The Royalists capture Beeston Castle

The reinforcements from Ireland enabled Hawarden to be recaptured for the King, and allowed an offensive to be mounted against other Parliamentary outposts. Captain Sandford of the King's Irish army and eight men armed with firelocks scaled the precipitous north face of the crag and siezed the inner ward of Beeston castle. The Parliamentary commander, Captain Steele, reputedly not a fighting man, relinquished control without resistance and entertained Sandford to dinner in his headquarters. Although Steele's garrison was 60 strong he was unsure of their loyalty. A large body of Royalists from Chester were outside the main gate and therefore, Steele negotiated surrender terms, marching out with colours flying and "honours of war" but leaving all the stores and valuables which had been sent to Beeston for safe-keeping. After arriving at Nantwich Steele was arrested, tried for cowardice and shot. Subsequently, Captain Sandford was killed in the Royalist siege of Nantwich, the Parliamentary headquarters in Cheshire.

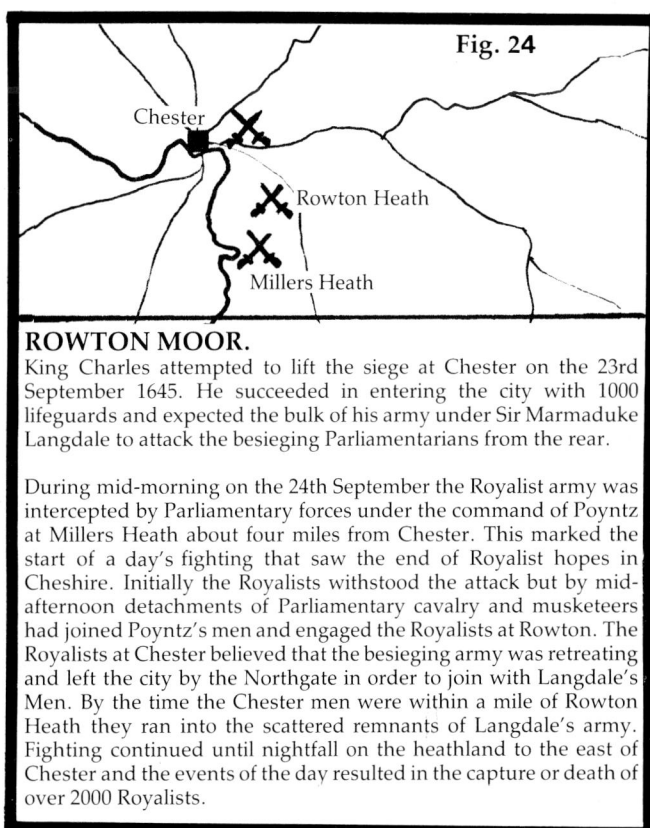

Fig. 24

ROWTON MOOR.
King Charles attempted to lift the siege at Chester on the 23rd September 1645. He succeeded in entering the city with 1000 lifeguards and expected the bulk of his army under Sir Marmaduke Langdale to attack the besieging Parliamentarians from the rear.

During mid-morning on the 24th September the Royalist army was intercepted by Parliamentary forces under the command of Poyntz at Millers Heath about four miles from Chester. This marked the start of a day's fighting that saw the end of Royalist hopes in Cheshire. Initially the Royalists withstood the attack but by mid-afternoon detachments of Parliamentary cavalry and musketeers had joined Poyntz's men and engaged the Royalists at Rowton. The Royalists at Chester believed that the besieging army was retreating and left the city by the Northgate in order to join with Langdale's Men. By the time the Chester men were within a mile of Rowton Heath they ran into the scattered remnants of Langdale's army. Fighting continued until nightfall on the heathland to the east of Chester and the events of the day resulted in the capture or death of over 2000 Royalists.

The Events of 1644

Byron's besieging army at Nantwich was defeated in January 1644, being outnumbered by Fairfax's relief force. The army of Ireland was shattered and the tide was turning in favour of Parliament throughout the North.

The King appointed Prince Rupert as Lieutenant General, with headquarters in Shrewsbury, requesting him to hold the Welsh recruiting grounds, win back the north and keep open the route from Ireland through Chester.

Rupert's forces temporarily ended the siege of Chester and Beeston and prompted the Parliamentary garrison to leave Halton. After Rupert's defeat at Marston Moor in July 1644, assessments were ordered for repairing the earth walls and gates and making portcullises at Chester. Halton was reoccupied by Brereton in August, and by late 1644 Chester and Beeston were again subject to siege (Fig 22).

Beeston's Royalist garrison did manage an offensive in December 1644, slipping out of the main gate and surprising a detachment of 26 Parliamentarians dining in Owen's House at the foot of the hill, killing all but two and setting fire to the house.

The events of 1645

The isolation of Beeston, Chester and other outposts prompted the Royalists to make further attempts at relief in 1645. Rupert's brother, Prince Maurice, failed to lure Brereton over the River Dee and thus relieve Beeston. Later Colonel Robinson at Holt Castle led an abortive attempt to lift the siege.

In March Rupert reached Beeston and Chester but then moved north taking the experienced Irish foot regiments. This encouraged Brereton to resume the Beeston, Hawarden and Chester sieges and, with the Royalist defeat at Naseby in June, the only hope of relief was from Ireland (Fig 23).

Chester and Beeston Besieged

By August 1645 Beeston was again entirely surrounded by ditches and a mount as cover for musketeers was built in front of the main gate. A barn was moved from Beeston Hall and rebuilt near the castle as a munitions store. In September some of the Beeston besieging force slipped away and helped to storm the defences of Chester. The north and east suburbs were captured which largely confined the defenders within the medieval walls.

Such was the importance of Chester to the Royalist cause that the King arrived with reinforcements on 23rd September. The following day his army was defeated at Rowton Moor and the King left the city to resist as best it could under the command of Lord John Byron (Fig 24).

The bombardment of the city walls had already caused considerable damage in September. Thirty-two cannon shots had breached the city wall near Newgate making a hole "the width of 10 men". It was repaired with beds and woolpacks. To relieve the pressure some of the garrison attacked the Parliamentarian headquarters at Eccleston and took some prisoners. To prevent a reoccurrence the

FOOT SOLDIERS OF THE CIVIL WAR
The foot soldiers of the Civil War fell largely into two groups, pikemen and musketeers. Musketeers carried matchlock muskets, bandoliers and swords. An early form of flintlock was in use known as a snaphance or firelock and was known to have seen service in the surprise assault on Beeston by Captain Sandford.

besiegers built a bridge of boats over the River Dee so that they could go back and forth across the river.

Chester's last hope of relief disappeared when a Royalist force, including Irish reinforcements, was defeated near Denbigh on 1st November. Chester was now effectively blockaded by Parliamentary bases at Pulford, Doddleston, Eccleston and Brewers Hall, cutting the supply links with Wales.

The Fall of Beeston

It was the depletion of food supplies which led the Royalist Governor to surrender Beeston Castle on 14th November. He and his men marched out with full honours of war. The Governor's horse was so weak from lack of fodder it scarcely had the strength to carry him. On entering the castle the Parliamentarians found "neither meat, ale or beer, only a piece of turkey pie, 2 biscuits and a live peacock and peahen". The surrender prompted Brereton to send a summons to Lord Byron and the Mayor at Chester demanding the "speedy surrender of the City, Castle and Fort ….".

The Fall of Chester

The rejection of this demand caused the siege to be intensified. Bombardment caused devastating damage in Eastgate and Watergate. On 10th December it was recorded "Eleven huge grenadoes threaten to set the city if not the world on fire". Morale rapidly declined and food shortages necessitated a vigilant guard on the garrison's horses. Lord Byron agreed to a peace conference on 30th January which led to the signing of surrender terms, these allowing the governor and garrison safe passage out of the city and Parliamentary forces took possession on 3rd February. The weakened population of the shattered city then fell victim to plague with over 2000 deaths in 1647. The city had paid a high price to earn the title "Loyal Chester". Parliament ordered partial demolition of the city walls, but it was not put into effect. The castle continued in use as a garrison headquarters and prison. Beeston and Halton were both subject to "slighting" and rendered useless for future defence.

Royalist Uprisings in Cheshire

With the final Royalist collapse the King was taken into Parliamentary custody. King and Parliament failed to reach an agreed settlement, and the conflict was renewed.

In the 2nd Civil War (1648) a plot to sieze Chester Castle for the King was foiled. The conspirators, who included members of the garrison, were shot by firing squad in the Corn market. In the same year an invading Scots army attempting to reach Chester was defeated at Winwick by Cromwell.

King Charles was then tried by Parliament for treason, and beheaded in 1649. The presiding judge at the trial was John Bradshaw of Marple Hall in Cheshire.

Charles' exiled son assumed the title, Charles II, and having organised a Scots alliance in 1650 invaded England in 1651 hoping to galvanize Royalist supporters in the North West. The Earl of Derby brought an invading force from the Isle of Man, but he was unable to raise much local support. Charles was finally defeated at Worcester, and the English Commonwealth was secure.

The Earl of Derby was imprisoned, tried and condemned to death at Chester Castle, following his capture after the battle of Worcester. He escaped but was recaptured and executed at Bolton.

During the Commonwealth some Royalist support was still evident in Cheshire. In 1659 Sir George Booth's rising was supported by the Mayor of Chester and the assembly. They ordered two companies of foot soldiers to be raised, but Booth failed to capture Chester Castle, and his rising received little support elsewhere in Cheshire. He was defeated at Winnington Bridge in August.

Although the English monarchy was restored in 1660, its power was henceforth curtailed by an unassailable Parliament.

GLOSSARY OF TERMS

The following is a list of some of the terms which occur in the body of the text.

BAILEY.	The defended outer courtyard of a castle.
BASTION.	An earthwork or walled projection from the line of a fortification.
CRENELLATION.	Fortification, a "licence to crenellate" was official permission to build a fortified structure. The "crenel" was the gap or embrasure in the parapet wall.
CURTAIN WALL.	A wall encircling a ward or bailey.
DOMESDAY BOOK.	A description of England, compiled in 1086. It provides information of the ownership and value of land.
DRAWBRIDGE.	A wooden bridge raised or lowered from a gateway by chains, ropes or counterbalance.
EARL.	A high-ranking British nobleman.
EMBRASURE.	See Crenellation.
EXCHEQUER.	An administrative department in charge of public revenues.
FEUDALISM.	Medieval European form of government in which a superior gave land in return for service.
FIRELOCK.	A self-igniting musket, shorter and lighter than the conventional matchlock.
GRENADO.	An explosive shell fired from a mortar.
HIDE.	Apparently a unit of taxation, based very loosely on a measurement of land.
JUSTICIARY.	An administrator of justice.
KEEP.	The great tower; main part of a castle of the 11th and 12th centuries.
MACHIOLATION.	An opening in the floor of a projecting parapet, or platform along the wall or above an archway, through which defenders could drop or shoot missiles vertically on attackers below.
MARK.	13s 4d (66⅔ p)
MERLONS.	Sections of parapet wall between the crenels or embrasures.

MOTTE.	A mound of earth usually found in castles of the 11th and 12th centuries.	
PERCH.	A measurement of length and area, usually of land; 5½ yards (5 metres).	
PLUMBER.	A lead worker.	
PORTCULLIS.	A heavy grill suspended by chains in vertical grooves in a gateway.	
SHELL-KEEP.	A stone curtain wall on a castle mound or motte.	
THEGN.	(Thane) An Anglo-Saxon nobleman.	
WARD.	A defended area.	

SELECT BIBLIOGRAPHY

Abbreviations

C.C.C.	Chester Community Council
H.M.S.O.	Her Majesty's Stationary Office
J.C.A.S.	Journal of the Chester Archaeological Society
L.C.A.S.	Lancashire and Cheshire Antiquarian Society

GENERAL WORKS

BARLOW, F.	The Feudal Kingdom of England 1042-1216	Longmans 1972
BROWN, R.A.	English Castles	Batsford 1976
EVANS, J. (Edit)	The Flowering of the Middle Ages	Guild Publishing 1985
HAYTHORNTHWAITE, P.	The English Civil War 1642-1651 (An Illustrated Military History)	Blandford Press 1983
PLATT, C.A.	The Castle in Medieval England and Wales	Secker and Warburg 1982
RENN, D.F.	Norman Castles in Britain	John Baker 1983
ROWLEY, T.	The Norman Heritage	Routledge and Kegan Paul 1983
	The High Middle Ages	Routledge and Kegan Paul 1983
STEANE, J.M.	The Archaeology of Medieval England and Wales	Guild Publishing 1984

WORKS RELATED TO CHESHIRE

BECK, J.	Tudor Cheshire	C.C.C. 1969
BU'LOCK, J.D.	Pre-Conquest Cheshire	Cheshire C.C.C. 1972
CHRISTIE, R.C. (Translator)	Chronicle of The Abbey of St. Werburg at Chester	Record Society of Lancashire and Cheshire Vol. 15 1886
DORE, R.N.	The Civil Wars in Cheshire	C.C.C. 1966
DRIVER, J.T.	Cheshire in the Late Middle Ages	C.C.C. 1971
HALL, J. (Ed.)	Memorials of the Civil War in Cheshire	Record Society of Lancashire and Cheshire Vol. 19 1889
HEWITT, H.J.	Cheshire under the Three Edwards	C.C.C. 1967
HUSAIN, B.M.C.	Cheshire under the Norman Earls	C.C.C. 1973

| KING, D. | The Vale Royal of England | 1656 |
| ORMEROD, G. | A History of the County Palatinate and City of Chester | 2nd Edition 1882 |

WORKS RELATED TO SITES

COLVIN, H.M. (Ed.)	The History of the Kings Works	H.M.S.O. 1963
COX, E.W.	Chester Castle	J.C.A.S. Vol. 5 1895 Parts 2-3
DORE, R.N.	Beeston Castle in the Great Civil War	The L.C.A.S. Society 1965-1966 Vol 75 76
HEMINGWAY, J.	A History of Chester	1831
MORRIS, R.H.	The Siege of Chester 1643-1646	J.C.A.S. 1924 Vol 25
OCHRIM, M.A.R.	Thomas Harrison and the Rebuilding of Chester Castle	J.C.A.S. Vol 66 1983
RIDGEWAY, M.H. AND CATHCART KING, D.J.	Beeston Castle Cheshire	J.C.A.S. Vol 46 1959
SIMPSON, F.	Chester Castle	J.C.A.S. Vol 26 1925 Part II
SIMPSON, F.	The Walls of Chester	1910
STEWART-BROWN, R.	The Cheshire Chamberlains Accounts	1910

PLACES TO VISIT

SITES OPEN TO THE PUBLIC.
Abb. O.S. Ordnance Survey

CHESTER CASTLE: AGRICOLA TOWER AND CASTLE WALLS
O.S. ref. SJ405658

Location.	Access via Assizes Court Car Park on Grosvenor Street. Exhibition on castle history in 19th c Guard Room.
Opening times:	Standard English Heritage.
Nearby.	CHESTER MILITARY MUSEUM, open all year. St. Mary-on-the-Hill. Redundant medieval church used as Educational resources centre. Has medieval glass and wall painting; open in afternoons.

KING CHARLES TOWER, THE WALLS, CHESTER
(a branch of the Grosvenor Museum)

| Location. | N.E. corner of the city walls. Houses Civil War Exhibition, Charles I reputedly viewed battle of Rowton Moor from this point. |
| Opening Times: | Weekdays and Sundays in summer, weekends in winter. |

BEESTON CASTLE
O.S. ref. SJ537593

Location.	11m S.E. of Chester between A41 and A49. Exhibition on History of Castle. Car park and toilets.
Opening Times:	Standard English Heritage.
Nearby.	Bunbury Church, 14th c tomb of Sir Hugh Calveley
OTHER SITES	with visible remains. Access may be limited.

ALDFORD
O.S. ref. SJ419596

| Location. | Midway between Chester and Farndon off B5130. Motte and Bailey visible from churchyard. |
| Nearby. | Farndon, 14th c bridge across River Dee. 14th c Barnston effigy and Civil War Memorial window at St. Chad's Church. |

DODDINGTON
O.S. ref. SJ709470

Location.   Between Nantwich and Woore, off A51. Pele Tower in Doddington Park.

DODLESTON
O.S. ref. SJ361608

Location.   S.W. of Chester between A55 and A483. Motte and Bailey adjacent to Churchyard.

DUNHAM MASSEY (WATCH HILL)
O.S. ref. SJ734874

Location.   Nr. Junction of A56 and M56 at River Bollin. Motte visible.

Nearby.   DUNHAM HALL (National Trust) Off A56. Open April to October. 16th c water mill in grounds.

EDDISBURY
O.S. ref. SJ553694

Location.   Close to Delamere. Minor road off B5152. Iron age/Anglo-Saxon defences visible.

HALTON
O.S. ref. SJ537820

Location.   Nr. Runcorn shopping city. Ruins on crag. Access from A558 and M56 Jct. 12.

Nearby.   Norton Priory. Monastic remains and museum. Open all year.

MALPAS
O.S. ref. SJ486472

Location.   Off B5069 from A41. Motte close to church

Nearby.   St. Oswalds Church 14th c Wooden Screens of Brereton and Cholmondeley Chapels. 18th c almshouses.

PULFORD
O.S. ref. SJ375587

Location.   Off A483 S.W. of Chester. Castle site nr. church by river.

SHOCKLACH
O.S. ref. SJ433508, SJ434509

Location.   Minor road S.E. of Farndon, at Castletown. Motte, and a defended enclosure on opposite sides of road.
Nearby.   Shocklach Norman Church 1m.

SHOTWICK
O.S. ref. SJ350704

Location.   N.W. of Chester, minor road between A550 and Sealand. Motte and Bailey visible.

MUSEUMS

CHESTER HERITAGE CENTRE

Location.   Corner of Bridge Street and Pepper Street. Exhibition on architectural heritage of Chester.

Opening Times: All year. Not Wednesdays October to March.

GROSVENOR MUSEUM

Location.   Grosvenor Street, off County Hall roundabout. Local material, particularly Roman period.

Opening Times.   Every day. Sunday p.m.

NANTWICH TOWN MUSEUM

Location.   Signposted in town centre.
                                Local history, Civil War display.

Opening Times: All year. Closed Monday October to April.

The Battle of Nantwich of January 1644 is re-enacted annually outside the town by the Sealed Knot. Nearest Saturday to 25th January.

Every effort has been made to provide accurate information regarding opening times etc. However changes may take place from year to year, and it would be advisable to check before a visit.

Typeset by North West Photoset, Liverpool.
Printed by Nelson Brothers Limited, Chorley, Lancashire PR7 1EJ.